Hats Off

Hats Off

Poems and Drawings

JOYCE GRENFELL

Compiled and introduced by

JANIE HAMPTON

John Murray
Albemarle Street

First published in 2000
by John Murray (Publishers) Ltd.,
50 Albemarle Street, London W1X 4BD

A catalogue record for this book is available from the British Library

ISBN 0–7195–6152 3

Typeset in 11 on 14 point Modern Extended

Printed and bound in Great Britain by The University Press, Cambridge

For Charlie

Contents

Introduction

Joyce Grenfell is fondly remembered as an actress and comedy writer but her first earnings were as a poet. Like many schoolchildren, she thought poetry 'dull stuff'. However, at the age of 25 she met the poet Elliot Coleman in America, fell in love with his verse and was inspired to write her own. She sent early efforts to her friend the comic writer Virginia Graham. Virginia secretly submitted one to *Punch* and a few weeks later Joyce was amazed to receive a cheque for ten shillings.

In preparing the first biography of Joyce Grenfell, to be published in 2001, I kept coming across poems among loose press cuttings, letters and notebooks – 'The Bumble Bee' was on a

The Bumble Bee

The Bumble Bee is oddly wrought,
Aerodynamically 's ought
To find 's quite impossible to rise,
But Bumble Bees don't know the rule,
For Bumble Bees don't go to schule –
They flies.

scrap of paper tucked inside her copy of John Betjeman's *Summoned by Bells*. In February 1941 she wrote of the loss of a notebook: 'It's got several jottings of poems that I can't remember. Once I've written down some idea or phrase it goes

out of my head because I know I've put it in a safe place. Only this time I didn't. Damn.' Even with this loss, there were more than enough to collect into a volume.

Joyce wrote in a funny, sad or wistful vein wherever and whenever the Muse took hold of her – on trains, waiting for the kettle to boil, or in her dressing-room at the theatre. She wrote about everyday incidents, using the same powers of observation that produced her monologues and songs. She wrote for fun and to explore her feelings: if her writing gave other people pleasure, so much the better.

The first world she describes is that of the upper class in the 1930s: débutantes just home from finishing-school and wives unwillingly in Scotland for the grouse shoot. *Punch* at the time carried advertisements for the Waifs and Strays Society; Chaventre Toupets, to overcome baldness – 'absolutely undetectable'; and Craven A cigarettes, 'made specially to prevent sore throats'.

In the early stages of the Second World War Joyce helped make sandwiches for lunch-time concerts at the National Gallery. Her reward was to listen from behind a screen, which inspired the sonnet 'On Hearing Myra Hess Playing'. Later she went on tour as a singer with ENSA, first around Britain and then to North Africa, the Middle East and India. 'Groans about Touring' was written while waiting backstage in a Nissen hut in Northern Ireland in 1943. Her poems about evacuated children, billeted soldiers and the loneliness of wives undoubtedly helped people to put up with the tensions of civilian life. In 1942 Virginia Graham wrote to Joyce on her birthday: 'Honestly, if I'd given one quarter the amount of joy you have given to all of us I would have nothing to complain of. I can think of no life more usefully & disinterestedly spent – & I find it particularly clever of you, now that you have attained such a large measure of success, to have changed not one morsel.'

The lyrical poems tend to be about Nature or Reggie, her husband for fifty years. Some of the later verses were probably written as songs but were never put to music.

Walter de la Mare was a close friend and agreed to comment on her poems. Of 'Children Evacuated' he wrote in a spidery hand, 'I still can't quite make up my mind about "rose noses" but "A clutch of cherubs clothed in coloured wool"is a bull's eye. I rather wished the grown-ups hadn't been there, but I suppose they had to be!' He loved the line 'The ragged rooks like tea-leaves in the sky'in 'March Day 1941', and advised Joyce to read her poetry aloud to herself as a test of its rhythm. Joyce wrote, 'He has the gift of making one feel almost intelligent oneself.'

John Betjeman was another influence and they held many poetry recitals together in village halls, on radio and in theatres. Betjeman would arrive at her flat in his battered straw hat, carrying a shopping-basket bulging with books. They would spend the afternoon reading each other their favourites – Thomas Hardy, A. E. Housman and C. Day Lewis.

Joyce drew all her own Christmas cards, often self-portraits in different hats. She had so many friends that she began as early as March, saying 'It's my form of knitting.' Some of the drawings in this volume were for commercial Christmas cards she designed in 1934. On holiday, whether in Suffolk or Sydney, she sketched the landscape, flowers and people around her. One year the Grenfells went on holiday to the Lake District with the Royal Academy artist John Ward and his wife Alison. John gave Joyce tips on improving her water-colours.

Some of her poems appeared in *Punch*, the *Observer*, *Country Life*, *The Times* and the *Christian Science Monitor*, but others were never published. Most of those that were, date from the 1930s and 1940s, but she went on writing poetry all her life. However, once she became famous for her songs and monologues, she felt less need to see her poems in print. Here, for the first time in one volume, are her best.

JANIE HAMPTON

Joyce Grenfell

Hats

Never wear a Pixie Hood
If your face is long and good.

And beware the Boyish Beret
When you're merely mild, not merry.

Do not sport an Eastern Turban
If you're simple and suburban.

Best not risk the Veiled Toque
If you are inclined to smoke.

Shun the all-revealing Bonnet
When your face has spots upon it.

Don't drown 'neath a Cossack Cap
If yours is a midget map.

Lastly, leave the Sailor Hat
If you look like This

Or That.

c. 1950

Monday Morning Mail

Darling Mum and darling Dad,
How are you? I'm quite alright.
Yesterday we won the match.
Can I have a flying kite?
And I left my skates behind.
Could you spare me one and six?
Atkinson has got a bike.
(He can light a fire with sticks.)
We had a treacle tart today.
I got E for last week's French,
But I wasn't quite the worst.
Shall I make a garden bench?
It will take a lot of wood,
But it's better than a box.
Matron says to let you know
That I need some woolly socks.
Meet you Sunday by the gym.
No more news. Love from Tim.

II

Dear Madam, in this morning's *News*
Is your ad. for General-Cook.
I am 40, fond of country,
Seven years with Col. Brook.
C. of E. and clean in person,
Honest, sober, fond of dogs,
I can manage any oven.
Ever truly, EMMY BLOGGS.

III

Dear Neighbour, I'm afraid
I must complain once more
About the noise your lovebirds make
Every morning, at half-past four.
And perhaps I'm not offending
When I mention gramophones –
Don't you think that yours wants mending?
Anticipating peace – JANE JONES.

IV

Cocktails, duck, Friday at seven?
Bimbo's flat. It will be heaven!

1937

Fetch down the Album

When I get uppish there's only one cure
To banish my posing and pride:
Fetch down the album, it's certain and sure
Quite soon to have dealt with my 'side'.

Look at the naked child flat on the rug,
Rolling its marble eyes, shining and smug.

'First little footsteps at Salcombe-on-Sea';
Don't look away, that baby is me.

Look at that creature with wires in her teeth!
(Thothe were the dayth when I learnt to say 'Pleeth'.)

Look at the chicken-wings moored to my hat;
How could my mother have dressed me in that?

Look at this cloche worn low to the lips!
Is it a wonder I never launched ships?

Ah that's done the trick; I'm quite humble once more,
All of my uppishness fled.
Don't try to squash me when next I get cocky,
Just fetch down the album instead.

1937

Farewell to Fun

I was finished off in Munich and I had a week in Rome
On my way from gay Vienna, via Florence to my home.
I'm really quite sophisticated, and I think you will agree
That I've got the polished glamour of a girl of twenty-three.
Oh dear! It won't be easy to become a child once more,
But I've got to be a débutante. It's such a frightful bore.

I'm seventeen next Wednesday week, and on that fateful day
My fond mamma will give a ball to start me on my way.
I've got a dozen party frocks in which to play the part;
All of them are white, of course, and none of them are smart.
So I'll have to give up lipstick and red varnish on my nails
Do without my cigarettes and brown Bavarian ales.
Oh, how shall I answer, when mere infants in the Guards
Ask what pack I hunt with, or do I play at cards?
Will I join a jolly crowd at Eton on the Fourth,
And will the 12th of August find me heading for the North?
Oh for those discussions with Hans and Franz and Paul
On Life and Love and Music – and Should we Marry at All!

    So say Goodbye to Munich
    Vienna days are gone:
    Forget the fun in Florence
    For work has now begun.

1937

Bringing up Father

'Do we have to go to the Mildewy-Maddows
Who live in a house which the Albert Hall shadows?
They will play very deep intellectual games
And drop some distinguished foreigners' names.
It wouldn't insult them for they'll never know,
So I really don't see why we bother to go.
　　Let's sup by our fireside instead,
　　　　My dear,
　　Let's sup by our fireside instead.'

'My love, we *must* go to the Mildewy-Maddows
Who live in a house which the Albert Hall shadows.
They are giving a dance for their daughter in June
And remember our Millicent's coming out soon.
So we've got to be nice – and you mustn't be silly –
To people who might send an invite to Milly.
    Leave your fireside you must,
        My pet,
    Leave your fireside you must.'

                    *   *   *

'Now *why* did we go to the Mildewy-Maddows
Who live in a house which the Albert Hall shadows?
I spoke to a duchess, whose eyesight had gone,
She took me for Geoffrey, her dead sister's son.
Our hostess mistook me for old Colonel Slaughter
Is this how I'm helping to launch our dear daughter?
    I won't leave my fireside again
        Oh no!
    I won't leave my fireside again.'

1937

Sad Plight of the Stout

I wish I were a handful, a pocketful of fun,
The Pixie type, the Fairy type,
A-laughin' in the sun.
I wish I were a Tinkerbell, to storm the heart of man,
A wondrous Never-Never girl, a female Peter Pan.
I'd love to be a plaything, an Elfin childish lass,
Instead of which I fear I am, the Large Heroic Class.

1937

Thames Valley Floods

Ornamental Waters
    Came within the night,
And where the garden dips a bit
    Is now a plain of light.

Where the emerald grasses
    Struggled with the stones,
The gentle waves were lapping soft
    In dulcet undertones.

Will it last till Easter?
    Shall we launch a boat
And give a boating afternoon
    With toast and tea afloat?

You shall wear your boater
    And I will wear my white
On our Ornamental Waters
    That came within the night.

1937

Cri de Coeur

Blessed Monday morning when the house is mine once more
And visitors with baggage have departed through the door.
I love my friends on Friday night,
On Saturday the same;
It's quite all right, I still delight
On Sunday that they came.
But blessed Monday morning, when I kiss them in the hall!
I must admit I like it best when no one's here at all.

1937

Martyrdom

How noble are the wives like me
Who dearly love the beach and sea;
We need our holiday for sure,
But have to spend it on a moor.
We have to clothe ourselves in tweed
To follow where our husbands lead.
We have to loiter in a butt,
And keep our mouths entirely shut,
Instead of sunning on the sand
Where conversation isn't banned.
When choosing our *costumes de sport*
To demonstrate *esprit de corps*,
We must revere the grouse on high
Whose gifts include the gimlet eye.
We dress in brown for *camouflage*
And quell our longing for the *plage*.
Of course some wives enjoy the fun
And play their part and shoot the gun.
Perhaps if we were sterner stuff
We too would like our pleasures rough.
Although we don't, we sweetly grin,
And take the recoil on the chin.

What wondrous wives some husbands wed,
We don't complain, we smile instead.
We love the sand and shore for sure,
But we are martyrs to the moor.

1937

29

Moving Pictures

Things I'd like to see again
From a window in the train.

Lacquered king-cups by a stream;
Georgian farmsteads painted cream.
A tidy woman sitting still
In a garden on a hill.
Moving rays of lettuce rows,
Willows black with nesting crows,
Cherry flowers, hanging high,
White against the stormy sky.

These are the things to see again
From my window in the train.

But until they learn to clean
The windows, all that's seen
Are the smears of grime and dirt
And the ashtrays over-flowing
On
    the
       floor.

1937

On Hearing Myra Hess Playing

Now when its great design is in my mind
In ordered beauty, natural and strong,
I see new visions where I once was blind
And hear the full perfection of its song.
Growing and growing clearer as it grows
Till all the walls are down and I am free.
Pictures there are: Wales, where the wild wind blows
Across from Cader, high above the sea;
And Carolina mountains; and a roar
Of coral willows on a silver night
Near Boston, flaming through the slanting snow.
These do I see, and love them at the sight.
But there's a wider view and it has stayed
Fast with me since I heard this music played.

1940

St James's Park in War-time

St James's Park in war-time is just as nice as not.
The geese are there,
The gulls are there,
The pigeons still are fat and fair,
And there are admirals everywhere –
A most distinguished spot.

St James's Park in war-time's less sombre than before.
The decent black
The city hack
Wore daily on his head and back
Has been exchanged by Tom and Jack
For uniforms of war.

St James's Park in war-time is still a place to see.
The birds are there,
The trees are there,
And still it's good to stand and stare
And sniff the slightly sooty air
And then go home for tea.

1940

Party

Oh Arthur, they're coming!
The party's begun –
How d'you do, Miss Montgomery,
Hello, Mr Dunn.
D'you know Major Wimble,
Sir Christopher Cook?
What fun, darling Dorothy,
How lovely you look!
Sir Wincanton Pluggley,
Mrs Borridge. (Oh hell –
Oh Arthur, Cousin Caroline's
Turned up as well.)
Mrs Mostyn and Mavis,
The Vicar, John Drew.
Hello, Cousin Caroline!
How nice to see you.

    So glad you could come
    How good of you to spare
    The time
    For it's just
    An informal affair.

Hello, Colonel Saxby,
Miss Bell, Mr Stone.
(Arthur, look – Cousin Caroline's
Dancing alone!)

How nice, Lady Bley,
Professor Crumb Teazle,
And how is Bombay?
Oh here's Mrs Buzbee
And Alderman Clews
(Arthur, now she is waltzing
Without any shoes.)
Mrs Biscuit, John Wilby.
(Don't look – near the door.
Oh Arthur, Cousin Caroline's
Full length on the floor.)

So glad you could come
How good of you to spare
The time
For it's just
An informal affair.

(I'm under control now,
Not making a fuss.
Let's pretend that she isn't Related to Us.)
Hello, Mrs Pomfret
And Councillor Brice
And Dr Smith Wellerby
And Matron – how nice.
(Oh heavens – a silence,
They're all in a ring.
Oh Arthur, Cousin Caroline
Is starting to sing!)

c. 1940

Sonnet

If ever I am rich enough to make
Generous gestures, let me hide my hand.
Let me give freely, lest my giving take
With it, freedom. Not the frailest strand
Of obligation must go with my gift,
Nor must the comfort glow of being kind
Be used to lend a foolish head a lift.
Grant I may bring a clear and seeing mind
To work in wisdom, giving with a touch
So light that never breath of power blow
Across the crystal of my sharing much
That is lovely. Pray I may mark and know:
Beauty dies like a linnet in a cage,
Beneath the bruising hand of patronage.

1940

All Clear 3 a.m.

'Good night,' they said, but it was day,
    Pale silver day – still colourless,
With trees and houses faintly drawn
    Against the country's silent grey.
The little fogs that rose to blind
    Wiped out the pictures slipping by
Until, quite suddenly, they went,
    Revealing distances behind.
Along the mist-wet roads we drove,
    White elder-flowers starred the hedge,
Home in the morning, sunless yet,
    I rode beside the one I love.

1940

Signs of the Times

A year ago, and long before,
I lightly scorned the wives who wore
A regimental badge or pin
In diamonds, gold, or even tin.
Now I am not above such trifles;
My husband's joined the King's Royal Rifles.

1940

Yokel Defence

'Think 'ers goin' ter rain, Jack?'
'Not afore the marn.'
'Shall us leave the 'ay to lay?'
'Yers, let's get us garn.'
' 'Ave you got yer armlet
Writ with L.D.V.?'
'Yers, I got me armlet.'
'Then come along wi' me.'

'Think 'er'll be a rich crop?'
'Yers, 'er's gude and thick,
Wer'll dry in the marning sun –
Dry up nice and quick.'

' 'Ave you got yer gun, Jack,
And a bite to eat?'
'Yers, I got a tidy snack
And me gun complete.'

'Think 'er'll be a long war?'
'Might – and 'gain 't might not.
'T all depends on this an' that
'N sort a crops 'e's got.'
'Time that we was off, man;
Got yer drop a tea?'
'Yers, 'tis in my little can.'
'Then come along wi' me.'

1940

39

Nursery School Evacuated

The empty village street curves up the rise
    In morning silence, early yet for trade.
The sun is warm and blue is in the skies,
    But last night's moisture lingers in the shade.
Beyond the curve high clamour, growing full,
    Precedes th' advancing tide of Under-Threes.
A clutch of cherubs clothed in coloured wool,
    Round heads, round eyes, rose noses and rose knees.
In tottering progress two by two they walk,
    Squealing broad Bermondsey of this and that,
Squeaking incessantly in infant talk
    Until they see the Airedale rout the cat.
He leaves the chase to mark the children there,
    Intrigued by the new company he's found,
Steps stiffly up to sniff th' carbolic air
    Likes what he smells and, yawning, stands his ground.
This is a moment might have been a year.
    What does he want, this giant black-and-tan?
Is this the time for friendship or for fear?
    For seeming nonchalance within a plan?
Held by a common awe the column stood –
    Round eyed, round-nosed, round-mouthed – a force at
    bay.
Authority at hand says dogs are GOOD!
    Quite satisfied the troop goes on its way.

1941

Men in the House

Two second-lieuts. p.g. with me
(Heigh-ho for the mudless stair!)
Two second-lieuts.
In big black boots
Bachelors both, sing-ho the free
Second-lieuts. (two bob and three).

Two second-lieuts., who shout and sing
(Heigh-ho for the bath mat dry!)
Two second-lieuts.
In nice new suits
Who lost their key and had to ring
(Two second-lieuts.) like anything.

Two second-lieuts. who bang and slam
(Heigh-ho for the ash-tray filled!)
Two second-lieuts.
The handsome brutes
I must confess that I, oh damn
(Two second-lieuts.), their victim am.

L'envoi
No matter how a batman goes
    To call his officer discreetly,
With bated breath and on his toes,
    He wakes the sleeping house completely.

1941

March Day, 1941

Taut as a tent the heavenly dome is blue,
Uncrossed by cloud or tossing twig or plane,
A measureless span infinitely new
To fill the eye and lift the heart again.
Deep in the wintered earth the shock is felt:
Glossy sweet aconite has shown her gold
And strong straight crocus spears, where late we knelt
To lodge their bulbs, are waiting to unfold.
The ragged rooks like tea-leaves in the sky
Straggle towards the earth with awkward grace;
A robin in a silver birch nearby
Thrusts up his carol through the naked lace.
I've known this day for thirty years and more;
It will go on as it has done before.

1941

Five Grey Pigeons

Five grey pigeons flew over the wood,
Arrowing down the green paved ride,
Sped on their way by a spanking breeze,
Taking the wood in a stride.
The coral sun stained pink their breasts
Hurrying down the evening sky;
Purple the bramble, red the ash
As five pigeons flew by.

1941

Holiday Snapshot

Nine of a summer's evening, warm and still,
I stood enchanted on a high Welsh hill.
Not far below me, neat from rock to rock,
Ran a red-haired child in a burnt-brown frock.
She was pursuing a difficult hen,
Lately escaped from a wire-patched pen,
Sang, as she ran and jumped different ways,
The turbulent tune of the Marseillaise.

1941

Tribute to a Treasure

A young hand-maiden served me once,
She house-kept with a pleasing grace.
Her temperament was calm and light,
Her very presence blessed the place.
She never got a message wrong,
She cooked and cleaned, she sewed, she swept;
She washed and ironed, she fed the dog:
She almost never over-slept.
Nor did she self-indulge in moods
To load my heart with weighty fears
By looking martyred, cross or hurt;
Instead she sang along the years.
Five happy years of carefree days!
And now my loved and leaned-on staff
Has, rightly, lain her apron by
To go in service with the WAAF.

1941

Soldier, Young Soldier

Soldier, young soldier, when fighting is past
What is your pleasure, young soldier, at last?

I'd like me a farm with a great span of sky,
And lights in the winders when evenin' is nigh.
And faith for my children and sun on my corn,
And joy for my woman from morn unto morn.

I'd like me to feel when the job has been done,
We'll all have a hand in the peace we have won;
That all of us strong by the pattern of war,
May build for the future as never before.

I'd like me to know that all over the world
A just flag of freedom was flyin' unfurled;
That none of the nightmare was really in vain,
That none of the nightmare need happen again.

1941

Note on the Passing of an Ancient Amusement

The child I was, sturdy in reefer blue
    With scarlet tam and gaiters just too short,
That child, unlike the present children, knew
    A disapproved-of but delighting sport.
Clear from the past imagination flames!
    Hoop-stick in hand (its hoop in adult care
Along the evening street; parks were for games)
    The player dawdled home – till Belgrave Square.
High railings that around the garden stood
    Turned then by magic to a giant harp,
Iron-strung with music kitchen-like but good,
    That spoke in London's mumble strongly sharp.
To make such music all you had to do
    Was drag the stick along the bars and run.
I still hear the sound! The feeling, too –
    Vibrations buzzing up the arm – was fun.

The parks and squares seem greener and more gay
    Since all the railings have been felled for war,
And though they gave some pleasure in their day
    London looks friendlier than it did before.

1942

At Night

We talked throughout the evening's changing light,
From day gold into pale metallic grey,
And saw the Cézanne cornfield settle for the night
Beneath the moon, cloud-swept in disarray.
We leaned upon the window sill and heard
The flutter of a sudden hurried bird;
The silver coinage on the poplar tree
Shook to the breeze and sounded like the sea.
Our ears shared all the little music then,
Our eyes gazed on the same untroubled view,
But as the passage clock was mumbling ten
I freely left her side and was with you.

1942

Seven Days' Leave: The Departure of the Soldier

No pools betray a towel remembered late,
The bathmat bears no giant soggy spore,
No matchstick, spill or stub defiles the grate,
The passage light burns wastefully no more.
All order reigns – an old maid's Paradise,
No smoke, no noise, no mess, no sign of life.
All's neat and quite and peaceful – at a price:
For I'm no spinster, dear heart, I'm your wife.

1942

Housing Problem

If you have dreamed, quite humbly, to reside
In two small rooms with bath and kitchenette
And just a *little* service on the side –
Dissolve your dream: the flat you want is let.
Mansions there are in Kensingtonian squares
Requiring merely six or seven maids,
A boy or two to carry coals upstairs
And ample cellar-room in case of raids.
Belgravia offers similar delights
And Paddington and Mayfair have a lot,
And distant Highgate lyingly invites
With 'Unique Res. Mod. Con. in Central Spot.'
Flats there are none; of palaces a glut.
The answer seems to be a Nissen hut.

1943

Groans about Touring

There's nothing chills one to the bone
Like standing hour by hour on stone.
Oh, glow-worm stove that yields no heat
That chokes the lung but chills the feet!
Oh, little dressing-rooms of tin
With inconvenient Sani-bin.
Oh, shadeless bulb hung high in space
Where never ray falls on one's face.
Oh, playhouse, cowshed, castle, hall
Oh, hangars (large) or Nissen (small).
But we don't mind nor do we care
As long as we're successful there.

Performing's alright, more or less,
But God defend me from the Mess.
The officers I get to know
Have never, *ever* seen the show.

1943

Portrait of an Actor

His small uncertain world about him spins.
He lives on words
Of praise, of gossip, of the party, of the play.
Like the reflection of water on a ceiling
He flickers,
Strong from a deep wave
Pale from a ripple.
Anxious to please as a child
But with an eye aware!
He has no deeps for solitude
But must be living in the light of company.
He hangs in wires, fine as gold and strong –
Even the world and daylight are a setting.
He lives on words – on praise –
They build him,
Torture him in criticism,
Deflating in an instant all bubble confidence.
He is a toy of words,
Two profiles done in Number Nine –
But where is the man?

c. 1945

Any Messages, Mrs Bolster?

Any messages, Mrs Bolster?

Well now, let's see.
Phome went when you were out.
Dint say oo he was
I arst im though because
You sid to, dint you?
But e woont leave no name,
Seemed like a shame.

No there wasn't no message.

O, someone or other run to say
Was you goin to the meetin
Because about the seatin
I tell er I dint know
And she says O,
I see.
And she ungup on me.

No there wasn't no message.

And a bit later on
Phome went again
And someone says it's me
And I says oo?
And e says you know oo darlin
And I tells im I wasn't you

You was out.
And e says you can't fool me with that act darlin
And I says to oom, do you wish to speak?
Bet e rungoff.
Wasn't it a cheek.

No there wasn't no messages.

c. 1946

Child by the Sea

About three, I suppose,
On the very edge of the pale grey sea
Jumping, flatfooted for splashes,
On each little curling wave
And laughing in ecstasy.
Starfish hands stiff with excitement,
Limp silk hair blowing across her eyes
Unnoticed. All the world lost.
Her bathing drawers (courtesy garment)
Are damp and low about her thighs,
The small brown body naked to the skies.
Complete absorption in the task at hand:
To jump on every curling wave
Just as it breaks upon the sand.

'Coo-ee, come back. It's time for tea.'
No response,
Only a new interest,
Stones for throwing at the sea.

1946

I'm in Love

I'm in love
Wiv a werry unsuitable man.
I'm in love
And it ain't a practical plan.
For there's an obstacle see,
I'm afraid there may always be,
There is an obstacle –
    He don't like me.

We work in the same greengrocer's shop,
We eat at the same café.
I say to misself 'This 'as gotta stop,'
But I can't seem to break away.
'E's ever so fascinating,
'E's ever so likeable too,
But when I say 'Hey, good lookin', what's cookin'?'
    'E says 'I don't like yoo.'

'E's so rude
And 'is 'eart is as 'ard as stone.
'E's so rude
He says 'Why can't yer leave me alone?'

Last night when we'd put the shop to rights
We goes to the caf' for a cup.
'E din't take no notice at all,
And I thinks ter miself: 'Might as well give up.'
'E sits there, not sayin' nuffink
And I'm wondering what 'e would do
If I should say to him 'I'm sick and tired of you great big
	hulking brute treating me like I was dirt under yer feet.'
When all of a sudden 'e says to me
	'I love you.'

1946

A Morning William Morris Might Have Known

Back to the Nineties for a morning's span
    A morning William Morris might have known.
Scene: a small lost river far in Suffolk
    With hanging wind-white willows overgrown.

Two boys are punting down the tunnel mile
    Of bronze-brown water, slowly moving on
Between the crowded banks where filtered light
    Lets in the needle rays of distant sun.

My town eyes see a dozen miniatures
    Like decorated chapter heads and tails,
Dear faithful drawings by a loving hand,
    A moth, a minnow, and some horned snails.

A spray of ripening bramble with its fruit,
    A kitten's pad of quilted pink and red;
Dark garnet-clustered elderberry plates,
    A wisp of traveller's joy with silver head.

A floppy butterfly dips at its own reflection
    In the mirror water's golden green.
Oh, sense of truth and timelessness! . . .
    The willows sigh: and midday strikes unseen.

c. 1949

In Retrospect

Now is the time for unmusical singing,
Now is the season of communal song,
Of roundel and carol
And Roll out the Barrel
By voices uplifted and *strong*.

All I ask very humbly,
In voice low and rumbly,
Is please could the tenors refrain
From having a go
At descants they don't know
Again and again and AGAIN?

1950

The Bumble Bee

The Bumble Bee is oddly wrought
Aerodynamically it ought
To find it quite impossible to rise,
But Bumble Bees don't know the rule,
For Bumble Bees don't go to schule –
   They flies.

c. 1950s

My Portrait

I am an impressionist portrait of me
Painted in nineteen hundred and three.
A misty miasma am I,
The result of a cult that disguises a lot
And sells for a price in the sky.

You will not see me very clearly –
Stand well back, half close your eyes –
I am an impression merely
Meant to tantalize.

See me here as 'Girl with Basket'
That's the basket, that bit's me.
Yes, it's sad to have a blob
Where your face should be.

Yes, the Ego suffers badly
For you see

I only occur as a blur
In the manner of Sickert;
I appear in a queer
Cloudy canvas by Steer.
(Hey-ho the Tate.)
I'd prefer, I confess,
To occur looking super
By Cadogan Cooper.
But elusive diffuse

In the Whisterlish way,
All silver and grey,
I only occur as a blur.

Yes, the Ego suffers badly
For you see

I only occur as a blur
In the manner of Monet.
Such is my Fate.
I'm addressed as the Best
Of the Courtauld Bequest.
(Hey-ho the Tate.)
I'd prefer I am sure
To be sculpted by Moore,
But in mist I persist
In the Whisterlish vein,
All mizzle and rain,
I only occur as a blur.

When you look at me,
It isn't me you see, you see
An impression done of me
Which mustn't look like me.
It's what the artist sees, and sees
Beyond whatever he sees in me.
Not what we see, you see
But what the artist saw, and he

Just doesn't see like you and me.
Yes, the Ego suffers badly
Still I haven't done too badly.
Hey-ho the Tate!

c. 1953

Father and Daughter

Oh, the sadness of the evening after tea!
The window-panes are pocked with tears
That blur the shrill viridian lawns;
The robin spills his little silver beads of song
And tears my heart in me.

Within the room my father sits
Existing in his chair
While Hindemith
(Bassoon and piano)
Unrejoicing on the Third
Bickers through the evening air.

The lead in the old man's feet and hanging hands
Weighs in my heart and in my head.
Where is that laughing creature, mountain high,
The dear companion of another day?

We walked together then, on Saturdays,
Went to the galleries and heard the Proms,
Saw the play from the pit,
And argued and walked and talked and walked and walked,
Father and daughter.
Liking the same poor puns,
Meeting on common ground.

1953

Walks of Life

Mrs Fanshaw walks with her nose in the air
And her eyebrows up in surprise.
'Who does she think she is,' they say,
'Going around in that peacock way?'
Mrs Fanshaw is totally unaware
Of her critics who take offence and stare,
And accuse her of sinful pride.
For Mrs Fanshaw isn't at all like that inside.

Mrs Mitchley walks sideways like a crab,
An apology on her lips.
'Poor little timid soul,' they cry,
'Mrs Mitchley must be terribly shy.'
Mrs Mitchley is very much on the spot
And shy is what Mrs Mitchley is not.
She likes to act as if she were,
Then people sympathize and commiserate with her.

Mrs Bampster walks with a jaunty bounce
And bounces about the place.
'She's a tonic alright,' they beam,
'Mrs Bampster is such a scream!'
Mrs Bampster's actually very low,
Her problems are far too big to show,
She faces life with flag unfurled,
As if she didn't have a single care in the world.

c. 1953

My Boy

My boy's bought a motor-bike
So we can make a move.
'It's time to spread
Our wings,' he said,
'We gotter get in the groove,' he said,
'With a couple of wheels to set us free
The whole wide world is ours to see.
You'll feel like a million
When you ride on the pillion
Of my motor-bike with me.'

My heart *sank* to hear him, for
I'm not what you'd call a sport,
But 'Okay', I says,
'Hooray,' I says,
Though I felt nothing of the sort.
I don't need speed
To widen my horizon
But he's my hero, so he is,
The one I keep my eyes on.

And all I see
As we rip along the road
Is the back of the boy I love.
Not for me
The beauty of the view.
I don't dare look
At what we're riding through.

I sit there
With my eyes shut tight.
I *daren't* look left nor right.
When we swerve around a curve.

And all I see
As we whip along the road
Is the back of the boy I love.
Every single Saturday
And every Sunday too
I fasten on my white
Crash helmet tight:
We gotter go somewhere new.
And when we get to where we've come to see
He says, 'We've just got time for tea.'
So we down a quick cuppa
Then we head straight back down the road
So as to be home in time for supper.
He wind-burns a lovely brown
As we hurtle through the scenery.
'Bang on,' he says,
'Hang on,' he says,
And I feel my face turn green-ery.

And all I see
As we nip along the road
Is the back of the boy I love.
I achieve
A sort of mental blank
As we skid ten feet
Then bounce along the bank.

And I pray
With my head well down.
I *can't* look left nor right
As we climb back on.
So I hold on tight
To the back
Of the boy I love.

It must be love.
I hate it so
But he only has to whistle
And away we go.

c. 1957

Song of Our Times

She wasn't just a lass in tweeds and twinset,
But an educated handsome cultured pearl.
A very pleasing sight, a brilliant mind too,
A formidable combination in a girl.

From University she went to London,
She married and was blessed with an Event.
And then the telly sent an invitation
To join a panel game, and off she went.

'What fun,' she cried, 'I'll buy myself a necklace
With candelabra earrings down to here.'
She kissed her husband and the baby, crying gaily,
'Aren't you happy this has happened to me, dear?'

At first the nation found her quite delightful,
She had manners and her wit was sharp and sweet.
She signed a contract for thirteen weekly programmes.
She would keep her head, stay firmly on her feet.

Of course she was determined not to alter
But she found she had to plan her life anew.
In demand for Brains Trusts, Garden Fêtes and Parties,
She spoke on many Liberal platforms too.

She went to every kind of Public Dinner,
And Women's Lunches somewhere in the sticks.
She made the headlines with her blunt outspoken sayings
And opined each day on how the nation ticks.

She said her bit about the state of British Railways,
A late train was her chance to scold.
She rapped the knuckles of the waiter in the Diner
And told Inspectors what she thought they should be told.

The more she saw of public life the more she liked it.
Soon she was recognized whenever she went out.
Then she began to take herself a little seriously,
Expected deference and threw her weight about.

She didn't heed her husband's voice as on she rattled,
She took to advertising – for a fountain pen.
She was on TV every time you turned your set on
Until the nation cried 'Oh Lord, not *her* again!'

One day at home she found a letter waiting,
Her husband flown – to Canada – to stay!
The invitations from TV, the Press and Public
Began to drop off and then faded quite away.

There is a Moral to this sad and sorry story:
It is better far to dwindle to a wife,
Than become a Bossy Boots and then discover
You're a half-forgotten VIP for life.

c. 1958

The Reason for Joy

The reason for joy
Must always have been known –
The moment of awareness
Of sun and son, of sudden light,
Of finding we are not alone.

The reason for joy
Is that Christ rose again
To show us that one's life is whole,
In spite of what the world's eye sees,
In spite of crucifying pain.
That is the point – the suffering
Was never blessed of itself,
Nor is the struggling human gain.

The reason for joy
And its satisfying grace
Is that the place we live in
Is the only heaven, and is now
Including all – including space!

The reason for joy
Is God, our very being
God is (therefore we are)
The very essence of
Our loving, living, seeing.

c. 1960

Playing the Joanna

'Let's get hold of Raymond
Let's get hold of Ray.
Sit him down at the old joanna
And make him play and play.
Raymond's always smiling
Lifts you out of your grump
Let's get hold of Raymond
To give the piano a thump.'

The hardest part is the old left hand
My chords aren't always clear.
But I get the old right pedal on
So as nobody can hear.
And so my fame has grown and grown
And I never charge a fee.
I feel that my gift is a rare one
Since I only play in one key.

'Let's get hold of Raymond
Let's get hold of Ray.
Sit him down at the old joanna
And make him play and play.
Raymond's always jolly
Raymond will do his bit
Let's get hold of Raymond
To give the piano a hit.'

c. 1960

A Commonplace

It's commonplace of course,
It happens every day,
Somebody's daughter is having a baby,
Unmarried and young – in the family way.
Somebody's daughter has made a slight error,
It happens every day,
There is sniggering and giggling behind closed doors.
It is different when the daughter is yours.

She doesn't love the young man,
She doesn't want the child.
She feels no shame, she says.
No blame, she says.
But when she's unaware
She looks so vulnerable and young.
I know she's muddled and in fear,
But she won't let me near.

Where did we lose touch with her,
Why did she drift away?
Were we too scared to dare to say
'We know that's right,
We know that's wrong'?
Did we care enough,
Or was it easier to let her
Have her own way?

She doesn't want our help,
She'll go it on her own.
She's got a plan, she says.
No man, she says,
She'd rather be alone.

What do we do now –
Be there to hold her hand?
Although we can't
We must pretend to understand.

c. 1960

Song of Gladness

I count my blessings as the years go by
I'm full to the top with gratitude.
Thank heav'n I say – at the end of each day
I'm a Pollyanna girl in my attitude.

    For I am
        Glad, glad, glad, glad,
        Glad and grateful too
For all the remarkable people and things
I never need be –
Or do.

I never need be a steeplejack
Nor a rugger blue,
Don't have to be a nudist and I needn't do judo.
I needn't sail a little boat

Around the world alone,
Nor need I be a vandal
And smash a telephone.

    For I am
        Glad, glad, glad, glad,
        Glad and grateful too
For all the remarkable people and things
I never need be –
Or do.

I needn't be an astronaut,
Or wrestle in the mud.
I needn't be a vampire
And down a pint of blood.
Don't have to be a stewardess
Upon the heaving seas.
I needn't do a Cossack dance
Upon my aching knees.

    I am
        Glad, glad, glad, glad,
        Glad and grateful too
For all the remarkable people and things
I never need be –
Or do.

1965

Flower-arranging

One bullrush akimbo
Ferns in a tureen,
By an old bit of driftwood
With pebbles in between
And a gladdy, recumbent,
With a cucumber (green)
Mean something peculiar –
I'd rather not know, oh
Please leave the flowers alone.

You torture the flowers
And bend to your will
The innocent daisy, the gracious lilies
But nature does better
With natural skill.
Here is an 'arrangement'
Called 'Paris in May'
A tin Eiffel Tower
Stood up in a tray
With a pink satin garter
Round a carnation spray
To suggest something 'naughty'.
I'd rather not say – Pray!
Please leave the flowers alone.

Just give me a jam jar with flowers stuck in
Or a rose in a toothglass or pot
To hell with arrangers who fiddle and fuss.
Away with the whole boiling lot.

c. 1965

Teatime Sounds

How beautiful the telly's thud
    Comes through the windows blaring.
No awful quiet stills the air
    And sets us all despairing.

With merry music magnified
    The ice-cream van comes loud
Between the houses echoing
    To call the telly crowd.

It blows, 'O— O— ANTONIO'
    In giant notes so clear
The kiddies at their telly tea
    Must all be sure to hear.

They bolt their paper packet soups
    And powdered custards jolly
Come screaming gayly to the van,
    'I wanna' n ice-cream lolly.'

c. 1965

Christmas Eve

Today with a long list of jobs to be done
As long as my arm,
And too many people in too many places pushing,
Christmas had lost its charm.
What with neon signs blazing and dazing
As they changed,
And nothing left in the shops . . .
No wrapping paper, tags or scarlet string,
Not a *thing* left . . .
And the wear and tear
Of trying to get from A to B
And no time to spare for transit –
Oh, I lost sight of Christmas.
'Well, it's not for me anyway,' I said,
'It's for the children.'

And I waited, tapping my foot,
On an island in mid-traffic,
While the lights deliberately stuck
To prevent me or anybody else
Getting anywhere.
'Oh Lor',' I said,
'Look at that terrible plastic duck
In a sailor's hat
Going by under a woman's arm,
What's that a manifestation of?
Thank heaven there are no more shopping days to Christmas.'
Christmas?
Oh, Christmas. I'd forgotten.
I looked along the busy city thoroughfare.
The holly colours in a hundred rear lamps
Made their small contributions.
Red buses rumbled by, loaded with individuals
And their packages and private plans for tomorrow.
A street band blew a carol.
The pink glow above the city
Hid the star,
But the street was bright with more than electricity
And through a crack in a man-made world
I caught a glimpse of the glory
And the good of Christmas.

c. 1965

Lunchtime Concert

Grey clergyman of eighty, next to me,
Lover of music though you well may be,
Yours was not a Christian way to act
This afternoon, and that, Sir, is a fact.
Crisp wheaten biscuits topped with slabs of cheese
Drawn from a paper bag upon the knees
May make an appetizing sort of lunch;
They also wreck the music, for they crunch.
And having crunched, the crumbs break off
And play old Harry with your dear old cough.
Grey clergyman of eighty, next to me,
Lover of Mozart though you seem to be,
I wonder how you heard a single note,
What with the crunch, and clearing of your throat.
As Nanny used to say so long ago:
You never did ought to of, you know.

c. 1970

Today

Some days start on a low dark note
But this morning when the sun rose
It wasn't one of those.

No wonder I feel wonderful –
The reason is very clear.
No wonder I feel wonderful –
You are here.
The day is very beautiful,
The reason is obvious,
The day is very beautiful,
All for us.
The cloudless sky is a butterfly blue,
The sun is as gold as the glory,
There's no doubt about it
There is going to be
A happy end to the story.
No wonder I feel wonderful
The reason is clear to see.
No wonder I feel wonderful
For I love you,
And wonderful, wonderful, wonder,
You love me.

c. 1970

Life Goes On

If I should go before the rest of you
Break not a flower nor inscribe a stone
Nor when I'm gone speak in a Sunday voice
But be the usual selves that I have known.
Weep, if you must,
Parting is hell,
But life goes on,
So sing as well.

Date unknown

Acknowledgements

The editor and publisher wish to thank the following for permission to reproduce poems:

Punch Ltd: 'Monday Morning Mail', 3 February 1937; 'Sad Plight of the Stout', 17 February 1937; 'Bringing up Father', 23 February 1937; 'Fetch down the Album', 3 March 1937; 'Thames Valley Floods', 10 March 1937; 'Farewell to Fun', 19 May 1937; 'Moving Pictures', 27 May 1937; 'Cri de Coeur', 14 July 1937; 'Martyrdom', 18 August 1937; 'St James's Park in War-time', 21 February 1940; 'All Clear 3 a.m.', 10 July 1940; 'Yokel Defence', 24 July 1940; 'Signs of the Times', 28 August 1940; 'Nursery School Evacuated', 2 April 1941; 'Men in the House', 20 August 1941; 'Holiday Snapshot', 22 October 1941; 'Tribute to a Treasure', 3 December 1941; 'Soldier, Young Soldier', 31 December 1941; 'Note on the Passing of an Ancient Amusement', 11 February 1942; 'Housing Problem', 14 April 1943; 'Child by the Sea', 25 September 1946; 'In Retrospect', 15 January 1950.

Claremont Fan Court School, Surrey: 'Party', c. 1940; 'Seven Days' Leave', 1942; 'Groans about Touring', 1943; 'Portrait of an Actor', c. 1945; 'Any Messages, Mrs Bolster?' c. 1946; 'I'm in Love', 1946; 'Hats', c. 1950; 'The Bumble Bee', c. 1950s; 'My Portrait', c. 1953; 'Walks of Life', c. 1953; 'My Boy', c. 1957; 'Song of Our Times', c. 1958; 'The Reason for Joy', c. 1960; 'Playing the Joanna', c. 1960; 'A Commonplace', c. 1960; 'Song of Gladness', 1965; 'Teatime Sounds', c. 1965; 'Christmas Eve', c. 1965; 'Flower-arranging', c. 1965; 'Today', c. 1970; and the illustrations.

Joyce Grenfell Estate: 'Sonnet', 1940; 'Father and Daughter', 1953; 'Lunchtime Concert', *c*. 1970; 'Life Goes On', nd.

The Observer: 'On Hearing Myra Hess Playing', 10 April 1940; 'March Day, 1941', 2 March 1941; 'Five Grey Pigeons', 28 September 1941; 'At Night', 6 September 1942.

The Poetry Society: 'A Morning William Morris Might Have Known', *c*. 1949.